Dear Parent:
Your child's love of reading starts here!

Every child learns to read in a different way and at his or her own speed. You can help your young reader improve and become more confident by encouraging his or her own interests and abilities. You can also guide your child's spiritual development by reading stories with biblical values and Bible stories, like I Can Read! books published by Zonderkidz. From books your child reads with you to the first books he or she reads alone, there are I Can Read! books for every stage of reading:

SHARED READING
Basic language, word repetition, and whimsical illustrations, ideal for sharing with your emergent reader.

BEGINNING READING
Short sentences, familiar words, and simple concepts for children eager to read on their own.

READING WITH HELP
Engaging stories, longer sentences, and language play for developing readers.

READING ALONE
Complex plots, challenging vocabulary, and high-interest topics for the independent reader.

ADVANCED READING
Short paragraphs, chapters, and exciting themes for the perfect bridge to chapter books.

I Can Read! books have introduced children to the joy of reading since 1957. Featuring award-winning authors and illustrators and a fabulous cast of beloved characters, I Can Read! books set the standard for beginning readers.

A lifetime of discovery begins with the magical words **"I Can Read!"**

Visit www.icanread.com for information on enriching your child's reading experience.
Visit www.zonderkidz.com for more Zonderkidz I Can Read! titles.

In your hands he has placed all mankind and the beasts of
the field and the birds in the sky. Wherever they live, he has
made you ruler over them all.
—*Daniel 2:38*

ZONDERKIDZ

Jungle Beasts
Copyright © 2011 by Zonderkidz

Requests for information should be addressed to:
Zonderkidz, Grand Rapids, Michigan 49530

Library of Congress Cataloging-in-Publication Data

Jungle beasts.
     p. cm.
  ISBN 978-0-310-72191-8 (softcover)
  1. Jungle animals—Religious aspects—Christianity—Juvenile literature. 2. Creation—Juvenile
literature.
  BT746.J86 2011
  231.7–dc22   2010037920

Editor: *Mary Hassinger*
Art direction: *Jody Langley*

13 14 15 16 17 /SCC/ 10 9 8 7 6 5 4 3 2

· · · MADE · BY · GOD · · ·

Jungle Beasts

CONTENTS

God made all animals.

Some of the coolest animals

can be found in the jungle!

One animal in the hot jungle is the …

PANTHER!

Panthers have lots of names.

They are sometimes called

pumas, mountain lions, or cougars.

Panthers are really big cats.

These fast cats catch deer to eat.

Sometimes they even eat alligator!

They can leap up to 20 feet!
This helps them catch food
they spot from trees.

A baby panther is called a cub.
Cubs are as big as a full-grown
house cat when they are born.

Another cool animal

in the hot jungle is the …

ANTEATER!

There are four different kinds

of anteaters.

The giant anteater is best known

and really is giant.

They grow five to seven feet long.

They can weigh up to 100 pounds.

Their long snouts help them sniff
out food because their eyesight is bad.

Anteaters can eat 30,000 ants
in one day.

Having a two-foot-long tongue helps!

Their tongues produce sticky saliva

which keeps insects from escaping.

But anteaters eat more than just ants.

Termites are also on the menu.

And if the anteater lives at a zoo,

he might eat mashed fruit such as

bananas and avocados.

Another fruit-loving animal

from the jungle is the …

ELEPHANT!

Elephants can eat up to 5% of their body
weight in one day.

That can be up to 660 pounds
of grass, leaves, fruit, and bark.

And they might eat 18 hours a day!

The elephant is the largest animal that lives on land.

They can grow up to eleven feet tall and weigh 7,000 to 13,000 pounds.

That's more than a car weighs!

African elephants have "fingers"
at the end of their long trunks.
These help them pick things up.

Even though elephants have big ears, they have bad hearing!
But those big ears have a job!

Elephants flap their ears like fans

to help keep cool

in the hot jungle.

A much smaller jungle animal

is the …

IGUANA!

There are many kinds of iguana.

Some are the green iguana and

the lesser Antillean iguana.

Some iguanas are small

like the green iguana.

This kind makes a good pet.

They can live in aquariums or cages.

You have to buy heat lamps to keep pet iguanas warm.

They are cold-blooded, which means their temperature is around 85 degrees.

Other iguanas grow up to 6½ feet long!
That's longer than some basketball
players are tall.

What do iguanas eat to get that big?

Iguanas are vegetarians.

Iguanas eat fruits, flowers, and leaves.

They love leafy vegetables such as

spinach and kale.

Iguanas come in many different colors.
They can be brown, green, or even red.
This helps them hide from animals
that might want to eat them.

God made all animals.

He made animals with fur and others with leathery skin.

And some of the coolest animals can be found in the hot jungle!